Write to I

Long ago, there were no cars or buses. How would you have traveled from place to place? Write two or three sentences about your ideas.

Write your sentences on another sheet of paper.

Fun Facts

- The first skyscraper was built in Chicago, Illinois. It was only ten floors high!
- Ancient Egyptian writing is called hieroglyphics. There are over seven hundred different symbols in hieroglyphics.
- Long ago, some homes had roofs made of hay.

Genre	Comprehension Skill	Text Features
Nonfiction	Alike and Different	• Glossary • Illustrations • Headings

Scott Foresman Social Studies

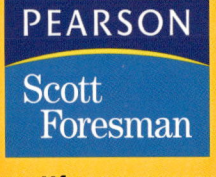

scottforesman.com

Then and Now

by Ellen Bari

Scott Foresman

Editorial Offices: Glenview, Illinois • Parsippany, New Jersey • New York, New York
Sales Offices: Needham, Massachusetts • Duluth, Georgia • Glenview, Illinois
Coppell, Texas • Ontario, California • Mesa, Arizona

Long Ago

Long ago, many people in the United States built houses made of wood. A **neighborhood** is a **community** of many houses built close together.

Today

Today, we still build houses made out of wood. We also use glass, brick, or steel to build houses. Many houses in the United States have running water and **electricity**.

Long Ago

Long ago, many people wrote letters by hand. They used a pen and paper. They sent these letters to family and friends.

Today

Today, many people also send e-mails from computers. The e-mails arrive fast!

Long Ago

Long ago, many people traveled on horseback. It took a long time to get places.

Today

Today, cars and buses travel on roads. Many highways make travel fast and easy.

Glossary

community a group of people and the place where they live

electricity a form of energy

neighborhood a place where people live, work, and play

cial Studies

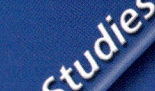

Then and Now

by Ellen Bari

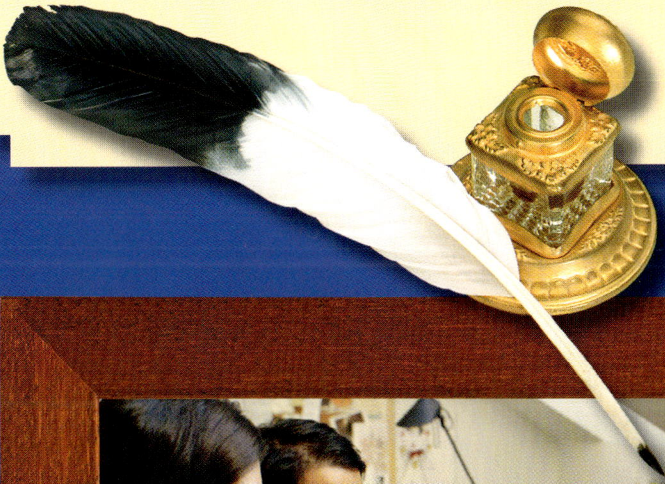

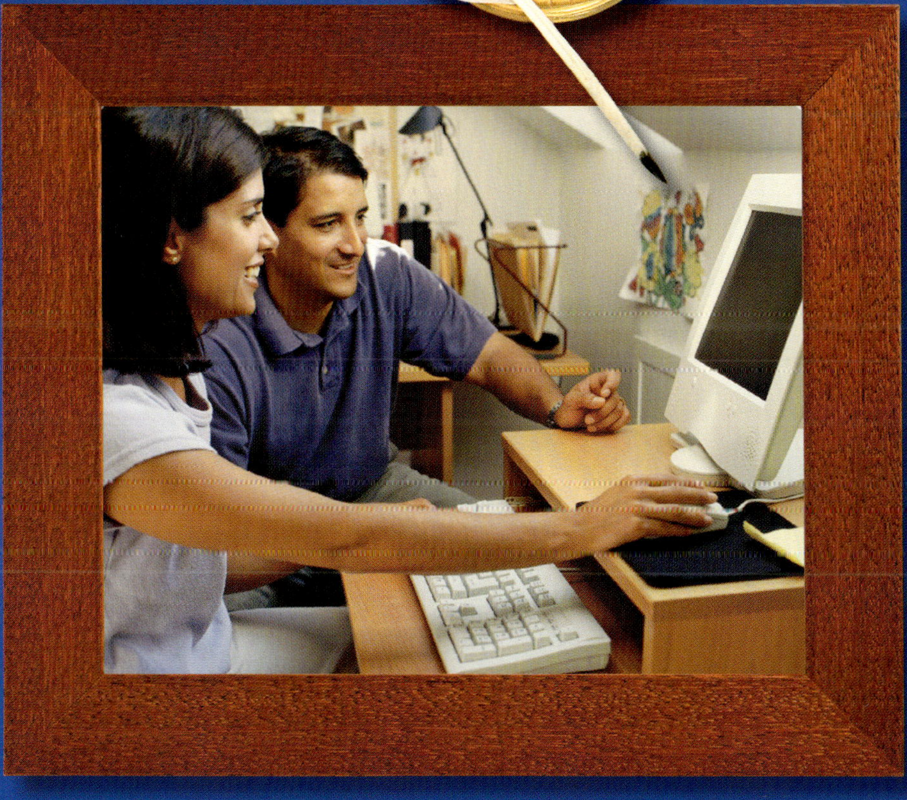

Many things have changed over time. We live in different kinds of homes. We travel and keep in touch with others in new ways. In this book you will read about these changes.

Vocabulary

neighborhood
community
electricity

Then and Now

by Ellen Bari

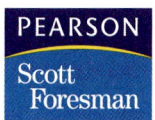

Editorial Offices: Glenview, Illinois • Parsippany, New Jersey • New York, New York
Sales Offices: Needham, Massachusetts • Duluth, Georgia • Glenview, Illinois
Coppell, Texas • Ontario, California • Mesa, Arizona

Long Ago

Long ago, many people in the United States built houses made of wood. A **neighborhood** is a **community** of many houses built close together.

Today

Today, we still build houses made out of wood. We also use glass, brick, or steel to build houses. Many houses in the United States have running water and **electricity**.

Long Ago

Long ago, many people wrote letters by hand. They used a pen and paper. They sent these letters to family and friends.

Today

Today, many people also send e-mails from computers. The e-mails arrive fast!

Long Ago

Long ago, many people traveled on horseback. It took a long time to get places.

Today

Today, cars and buses travel on roads. Many highways make travel fast and easy.

Glossary

community a group of people and the place where they live

electricity a form of energy

neighborhood a place where people live, work, and play

Then and Now

by Ellen Bari

Editorial Offices: Glenview, Illinois • Parsippany, New Jersey • New York, New York
Sales Offices: Needham, Massachusetts • Duluth, Georgia • Glenview, Illinois
Coppell, Texas • Ontario, California • Mesa, Arizona

Long Ago

Long ago, many people in the United States built houses made of wood. A **neighborhood** is a **community** of many houses built close together.

Today

Today, we still build houses made out of wood. We also use glass, brick, or steel to build houses. Many houses in the United States have running water and **electricity**.

Long Ago

Long ago, many people wrote letters by hand. They used a pen and paper. They sent these letters to family and friends.

Today

Today, many people also send e-mails from computers. The e-mails arrive fast!

Long Ago

Long ago, many people traveled on horseback. It took a long time to get places.

Today

Today, cars and buses travel on roads. Many highways make travel fast and easy.

Glossary

community a group of people and the place where they live

electricity a form of energy

neighborhood a place where people live, work, and play

Write to It!

Long ago, there were no cars or buses. How would you have traveled from place to place? Write two or three sentences about your ideas.

Write your sentences on another sheet of paper.

Every effort has been made to secure permission and provide appropriate credit for photographic material. The publisher deeply regrets any omission and pledges to correct errors called to its attention in subsequent editions.

Unless otherwise acknowledged, all photographs are the property of Scott Foresman, a division of Pearson Education.

Photo locators denoted as follows: Top (T), Center (C), Bottom (B), Left (L), Right (R), Background (Bkgd)

Opener: Getty Royalty; 1 Getty Royalty; 2 Corbis Media; 3 Getty Royalty; 4 Getty Royalty; 7 Corbis Media; 8 Getty Royalty, Robert Harding

Many things have changed over time. We live in different kinds of homes. We travel and keep in touch with others in new ways. In this book you will read about these changes.

Vocabulary

neighborhood
community
electricity

Then and Now

by Ellen Bari

Editorial Offices: Glenview, Illinois • Parsippany, New Jersey • New York, New York
Sales Offices: Needham, Massachusetts • Duluth, Georgia • Glenview, Illinois
Coppell, Texas • Ontario, California • Mesa, Arizona

Long Ago

Long ago, many people in the United States built houses made of wood. A **neighborhood** is a **community** of many houses built close together.

Today

Today, we still build houses made out of wood. We also use glass, brick, or steel to build houses. Many houses in the United States have running water and **electricity**.

Long Ago

Long ago, many people wrote letters by hand. They used a pen and paper. They sent these letters to family and friends.

Today

Today, many people also send e-mails from computers. The e-mails arrive fast!

Long Ago

Long ago, many people traveled on horseback. It took a long time to get places.

Today

Today, cars and buses travel on roads. Many highways make travel fast and easy.

Glossary

community a group of people and the place where they live

electricity a form of energy

neighborhood a place where people live, work, and play

Write to It!

Long ago, there were no cars or buses. How would you have traveled from place to place? Write two or three sentences about your ideas.

Write your sentences on another sheet of paper.

Every effort has been made to secure permission and provide appropriate credit for photographic material. The publisher deeply regrets any omission and pledges to correct errors called to its attention in subsequent editions.

Unless otherwise acknowledged, all photographs are the property of Scott Foresman, a division of Pearson Education.

Photo locators denoted as follows: Top (T), Center (C), Bottom (B), Left (L), Right (R), Background (Bkgd)

Opener: Getty Royalty; 1 Getty Royalty; 2 Corbis Media; 3 Getty Royalty; 4 Getty Royalty; 7 Corbis Media; 8 Getty Royalty, Robert Harding

Many things have changed over time. We live in different kinds of homes. We travel and keep in touch with others in new ways. In this book you will read about these changes.

Vocabulary

neighborhood
community
electricity

Then and Now

by Ellen Bari

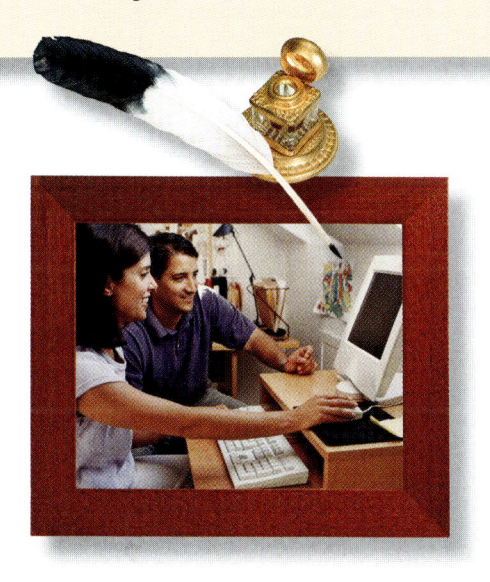

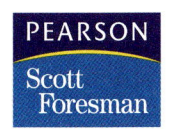

PEARSON
Scott Foresman

Editorial Offices: Glenview, Illinois • Parsippany, New Jersey • New York, New York
Sales Offices: Needham, Massachusetts • Duluth, Georgia • Glenview, Illinois
Coppell, Texas • Ontario, California • Mesa, Arizona

Long Ago

Long ago, many people in the United States built houses made of wood. A **neighborhood** is a **community** of many houses built close together.

Today

Today, we still build houses made out of wood. We also use glass, brick, or steel to build houses. Many houses in the United States have running water and **electricity**.

Long Ago

Long ago, many people wrote letters by hand. They used a pen and paper. They sent these letters to family and friends.

Today

Today, many people also send e-mails from computers. The e-mails arrive fast!

Long Ago

Long ago, many people traveled on horseback. It took a long time to get places.

Today

Today, cars and buses travel on roads. Many highways make travel fast and easy.

Glossary

community a group of people and the place where they live

electricity a form of energy

neighborhood a place where people live, work, and play

Write to It!

Long ago, there were no cars or buses. How would you have traveled from place to place? Write two or three sentences about your ideas.

Write your sentences on another sheet of paper.

Every effort has been made to secure permission and provide appropriate credit for photographic material. The publisher deeply regrets any omission and pledges to correct errors called to its attention in subsequent editions.

Unless otherwise acknowledged, all photographs are the property of Scott Foresman, a division of Pearson Education.

Photo locators denoted as follows: Top (T), Center (C), Bottom (B), Left (L), Right (R), Background (Bkgd)

Opener: Getty Royalty; 1 Getty Royalty; 2 Corbis Media; 3 Getty Royalty; 4 Getty Royalty; 7 Corbis Media; 8 Getty Royalty, Robert Harding

Many things have changed over time. We live in different kinds of homes. We travel and keep in touch with others in new ways. In this book you will read about these changes.

Vocabulary

neighborhood
community
electricity

Then and Now

by Ellen Bari

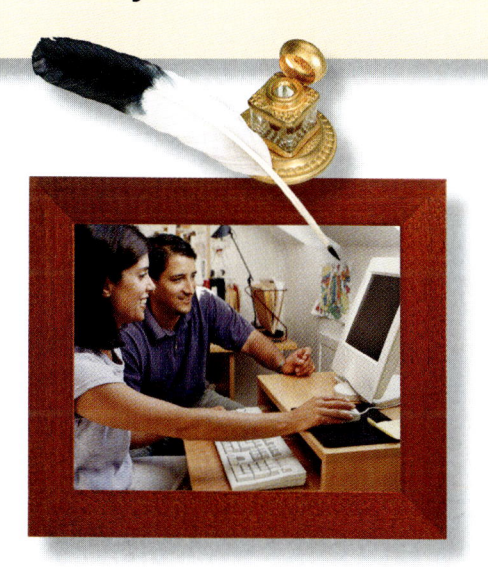

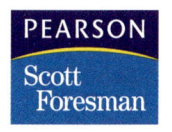

PEARSON
Scott Foresman

Editorial Offices: Glenview, Illinois • Parsippany, New Jersey • New York, New York
Sales Offices: Needham, Massachusetts • Duluth, Georgia • Glenview, Illinois
Coppell, Texas • Ontario, California • Mesa, Arizona

Long Ago

Long ago, many people in the United States built houses made of wood. A **neighborhood** is a **community** of many houses built close together.

Today

Today, we still build houses made out of wood. We also use glass, brick, or steel to build houses. Many houses in the United States have running water and **electricity**.

Long Ago

Long ago, many people wrote letters by hand. They used a pen and paper. They sent these letters to family and friends.

Today

Today, many people also send e-mails from computers. The e-mails arrive fast!

Long Ago

Long ago, many people traveled on horseback. It took a long time to get places.

Today

Today, cars and buses travel on roads. Many highways make travel fast and easy.

Glossary

community a group of people and the place where they live

electricity a form of energy

neighborhood a place where people live, work, and play

Write to It!

Long ago, there were no cars or buses. How would you have traveled from place to place? Write two or three sentences about your ideas.

Write your sentences on another sheet of paper.

Every effort has been made to secure permission and provide appropriate credit for photographic material. The publisher deeply regrets any omission and pledges to correct errors called to its attention in subsequent editions.

Unless otherwise acknowledged, all photographs are the property of Scott Foresman, a division of Pearson Education.

Photo locators denoted as follows: Top (T), Center (C), Bottom (B), Left (L), Right (R), Background (Bkgd)

Opener: Getty Royalty; 1 Getty Royalty; 2 Corbis Media; 3 Getty Royalty; 4 Getty Royalty; 7 Corbis Media; 8 Getty Royalty, Robert Harding

Fun Facts

- The first skyscraper was built in Chicago, Illinois. It was only ten floors high!
- Ancient Egyptian writing is called hieroglyphics. There are over seven hundred different symbols in hieroglyphics.
- Long ago, some homes had roofs made of hay.

Genre	Comprehension Skill	Text Features
Nonfiction	Alike and Different	• Glossary • Illustrations • Headings

Scott Foresman Social Studies

PEARSON
Scott Foresman

scottforesman.com

ISBN 0-328-14793-1